A Traveler's Guide Beer Tourism in Munich

By Paris Finch

Table of Contents

Introduction

I remember well my first trip to Germany in 1995, and after landing at Frankfurt airport, I traveled to Heidelberg for my first hotel night. That day, in a square in Heidelberg, I had my first German beer that was drawn directly from the tap. It was a Hefe-Weise bier, with yeast particles floating throughout the glass. The beer sat in front of me like a trophy in the sunshine while a studied the setting of consuming my first German beer experience. The taste of the beer was enriching, it tasted alive, with flavors I never imagined before while drinking the golden beverage. From that point on, I may sure to sample the local beers, which were all plentiful and delightful.

My trip eventually landed me in Munich, where the town was quiet and empty in the surrounding area of my hotel. I later learned that the local football team had just won the championship and as I approached the city center, the crowds grew along with the feeling of good will and fellowship. Of course, the beer was flowing. Every beer hall, every restaurant and every corner pub were overflowing with celebration and good spirits. A that time, I understood that I had a special connection with this city, this culture, and the local population.

Later in my professional career, I came to need to travel to Munich on regular occasions for work meetings and other business. This afforded me the opportunity to learn more about the city, the culture and to know the people very well. Navigating from the airport to the S-Bahn, to the city center became an automatic function for me. In addition, I had a terrific opportunity to experience those sights and sounds of the city, all the important sites and the supporting history of this city. This included sampling the many beers and food of the Bavarian capital. This allowed me to learn much and to set my favorites of activities or food/beer and to share that with others during my visits. I became to understand that I knew much about this city, but this was all in my head, never written down. Knowing all these facts about a city and finding that tourists would consistently stop and ask me directions or suggestions. When this experience started to happen with Germans, I realized that I must walk through the city center with a look of confidence and happiness.

Circle to recent times, my oldest daughter expressed an interest in attending the next Oktoberfest and asked if I would help with guiding her and making travel arrangements. This is what brought me to document all the information contained in this book so she, her friends, and any reader can learn and then put these learning forward to better enjoy this great city.

I have traveled all around the world, to every major city and even to some back roads and jungle locations, so I have experienced and saw so much of this planet. When people ask me about where my favorite place is to travel in the world, I never hesitate. The answer is Munich, Germany. München.

Munich, Germany

Munich, (or München), named for "Home of the Monks," the capital city of Bavaria in Germany, is a vibrant metropolis known for its rich history, cultural heritage, and modern amenities. Here is a summary of Munich's key aspects:

Cultural Hub: Munich blends a deep-rooted Bavarian tradition with a modern, cosmopolitan vibe. It is renowned for its cultural offerings, including world-class museums, art galleries, theaters, and music venues.

Historical Landmarks: The city boasts stunning architectural landmarks like Marienplatz, home to the famous Glockenspiel, and iconic buildings such as Frauenkirche (Cathedral of Our Dear Lady) and Nymphenburg Palace, reflecting Munich's royal heritage.

Beer Culture: Munich is synonymous with beer culture. It is home to legendary beer halls like the Hofbräuhaus and Augustiner Bräustuben, offering an authentic Bavarian beer-drinking experience, especially during the globally celebrated Oktoberfest.

Natural Beauty: Despite being a bustling city, Munich offers green spaces like Englischer Garten, one of the world's largest urban parks, and the serene Nymphenburg Park, providing tranquility amid the urban landscape.

Economic Powerhouse: Munich is a thriving economic center with a robust economy fueled by industries such as technology, finance, and manufacturing. It hosts multinational companies, making it a hub for innovation and business.

Culinary Delights: Bavarian cuisine shines in Munich with hearty dishes like weißwurst (white sausage), pretzels, and pork knuckles served in traditional beer halls, complemented by a rich array of international dining options.

Festivals and Events: Beyond Oktoberfest, Munich hosts a myriad of cultural events, including Christmas markets, music festivals, and cultural celebrations throughout the year.

Public Transport and Infrastructure: Munich's efficient public transportation system, including the U-Bahn, S-Bahn, and trams, makes exploring the city and its surrounding areas convenient for locals and visitors alike.

Munich's blend of history, modernity, culture, and innovation makes it an enticing destination. Visitors are drawn to its vibrant atmosphere, rich heritage, and diverse offerings, making it a city that caters to a wide range of interests and tastes.

Bavaria, Germany

Bavaria, or in German, "Bayern," is a federal state (Bundesland) in the southeastern part of Germany. It is the largest state by land area and is known for its distinct cultural identity, rich history, stunning landscapes, and vibrant traditions. Here are some key aspects of Bavaria:

Cultural Heritage: Bavaria has a strong cultural identity deeply rooted in its history. It is known for its traditional Bavarian dress (dirndls and lederhosen), folk music, dances, and distinctive festivals like Oktoberfest.

Scenic Landscapes: The region is characterized by its diverse landscapes, including the Bavarian Alps in the south, picturesque lakes like Lake Constance and Lake Chiemsee, and the Danube River running through the region.

Rich History: Bavaria has a storied past, with a legacy that includes the Bavarian monarchy and iconic historical figures like King Ludwig II, known for his castles like Neuschwanstein and Herrenchiemsee.

Economic Significance: Bavaria is an economic powerhouse in Germany, home to multinational corporations, high-tech industries, and a thriving economy. Cities like Munich, Nuremberg, and Augsburg are key centers for business and innovation.

Beer and Cuisine: Bavaria is famous for its beer culture. The region boasts numerous breweries, beer gardens, and traditional beer halls where locals and visitors gather to enjoy Bavarian brews and hearty cuisine like weißwurst, pretzels, and pork dishes.

Cultural Sites: Bavaria is dotted with historical landmarks, palaces, churches, and museums highlighting its rich heritage. Landmarks such as Nymphenburg Palace, the Residenz in Munich, and the Walhalla memorialize Bavaria's history and culture.

Bavaria holds a special place in Germany, renowned for its blend of natural beauty, cultural traditions, historical significance, and economic vitality. Its unique identity and contributions make it a captivating region to explore within Germany.

Bavarian Beers

Bavaria, known for its rich beer culture, offers a diverse range of popular beer styles, each with its unique characteristics and flavors. Some of the most famous types of beers found in Bavaria include:

Weißbier (Wheat Beer): This style is a Bavarian specialty known for its cloudy appearance and fruity, spicy flavors. Weißbier is often served in tall, slender glasses and is a refreshing choice, especially during warmer months. Never drink it from the bottle and generally consume in the Wirtshaus. Weissbier is the traditional morning beer and is usually drunk with Weisswurst for breakfast. Popular with anyone who does not need to go back to work afterwards. Workaholics and competitive athletes choose the alcohol-free version.

Helles: A pale lager characterized by its golden color and balanced taste. Helles is a light, malty beer that is crisp and easy to drink, commonly enjoyed in beer gardens and at social gatherings. Helles is consumed anywhere that is "gemütlich" (cozy) such as in a beer garden, a beer hall, in the Bavarian corner pub – the "Boazn," by the Isar, in the Wirtshaus, in front of the TV. It is liquid democracy. Everyone drinks it! If you are in a Wirtshaus and order "a beer," you will always be served a Helles.

Dunkel: A darker lager with a richer, malty flavor profile. Dunkel beers have a deep amber to dark brown color and offer a more robust taste compared to Helles. Dunkels are consumed mostly in the Wirtshaus (tavern), mainly with a hearty meal and preferably in winter. It goes well with game, duck, and roast pork. Consumed by locals, often of relatively advanced years and always with a special knowledge of Bavarian cuisine. Usually, you will only drink one Dunkel and then switch to Helles.

Pilsner: While more associated with northern Germany, Pilsners are also brewed in Bavaria. This pale lager has a noticeable hoppy bitterness, a golden color, and a clean, crisp taste. Pils is drunk in the pub, traditionally in the "Boazn" (local/corner pub), but also in restaurants. It is a classic beer on tap, and is often poured very slowly, which is why it is less carbonated than other beers. Consumed by those that like a finely hopped favor.

Bock: Bock beers are stronger, malty lagers that vary from pale gold to dark brown in color. They often have a higher alcohol content and are enjoyed during special occasions, especially the stronger Doppelbock.

Rauchbier: Originating from Bamberg in Franconia (part of Bavaria), Rauchbier is known for its smoky flavor imparted by drying malt over an open flame.

It has a distinctive taste appreciated by enthusiasts.

Kellerbier/Zwickelbier: Unfiltered, unpasteurized lagers with a cloudy appearance and a fuller taste due to retained yeast and proteins. They are often served directly from the brewery's cellar (Keller).

Each of these beer styles contributes to Bavaria's rich brewing heritage, offering a wide range of flavors and experiences for beer enthusiasts. Whether enjoying a refreshing Weißbier in a beer garden or savoring the malty notes of a Dunkel, Bavaria's diverse beer culture has something to offer for every palate.

Beer Vessels – Glasses and Steins

In Munich, beer is not only celebrated for its taste but also for the vessels it is served in. Different types of beer in Munich are often associated with specific beer glasses or steins, each designed to complement the beer's aroma, taste, and overall drinking experience. Here are some common beer glasses you might encounter in Munich:

Mass (Maß): The classic beer stein used during Oktoberfest and in many beer gardens. It is a hefty glass mug that typically holds one liter of beer, allowing for a hearty and communal drinking experience.

Weißbier Glass: A tall, slender glass with a narrow top used for wheat beers (Weißbier). Its shape helps maintain the beer's frothy head and allows drinkers to appreciate the beer's cloudy appearance.

Stange: A slender, cylindrical glass used for serving Kölsch, a light and crisp beer style from Cologne. This glass emphasizes the beer's delicate flavors and encourages slow sipping.

Pokal: A stemmed glass with a wide bowl, often used for serving premium or specialty beers. Its design highlights the beer's color and aroma while allowing for a more refined drinking experience.

Tulip Glass: Like the Pokal, the tulip-shaped glass is used for aromatic beers, especially those with strong scents. It traps the beer's aroma and concentrates it near the top for better appreciation.

Pilsner Glass: Though more common in other regions of Germany, you might find Pilsner glasses in Munich. They are tall and tapered to highlight the beer's clarity and effervescence.

These glasses not only serve practical purposes but also contribute to the cultural experience of enjoying beer in Munich. Each glass is tailored to specific beer styles, enhancing the drinking experience, and allowing beer enthusiasts to appreciate the nuances of different brews. Locals will store their beer stein at the beer hall in a secured locker. When local is done drinking beer for the night, they rinse out the beer stein in a sink and store in their personal locker.

Beer Drinking Tradition and Etiquette

In Munich, beer drinking is steeped in tradition and etiquette. Understanding and respecting these customs can enhance your experience and help you immerse yourself in the local beer culture. Here are some beer-drinking etiquette tips in Munich:

Prost! (Cheers!): When clinking bottom of glasses for a toast, it is customary to make eye contact with everyone involved. Lift your glass and say "Prost!" before taking a sip.

Ordering Beer: In beer gardens or halls, find a spot at a communal table and signal the server by making eye contact or raising your hand politely. Beer is often served in liters (Mass) or half-liters (Halbe).

Seating Etiquette: If the beer garden or hall is crowded and you are looking for a seat, it is acceptable to ask if the seats at a communal table are taken. Most often, these spaces are shared.

Paying for Rounds: In groups, it is common for individuals to take turns buying rounds of beer. When it is your turn, offer to buy a round for the table.

Tipping: Tipping in Munich is appreciated but not mandatory. You can round up the bill or leave a small tip as a gesture of appreciation for good service.

Respect the Beer: Bavarians take their beer seriously. Avoid mixing beers or adding anything to the beer, such as ice. Also, never clink glasses with a non-alcoholic beverage against a beer glass during a toast.

Closing Time: Beer gardens and halls have specific closing times. Respect these and plan your visit accordingly.

Glass Handling: Hold the beer glass by the handle (if it has one) or by the body of the glass to avoid warming the beer with your hands.

Conversation and Socializing: Beer drinking in Munich is often a social affair. Engage in conversations with those around you, especially at communal tables, and enjoy the camaraderie.

Know Your Limits: Pace yourself while drinking, especially if you are indulging in the stronger Bavarian beers. Drink responsibly and know when it is time to stop.

Following these customs not only respects the local traditions but also enhances your experience, allowing you to immerse yourself in Munich's rich beer culture and enjoy the convivial atmosphere of its beer gardens and halls.

Beer Hall Music

Beer hall music in Munich, especially during traditional events like Oktoberfest or in various beer halls, typically consists of lively and spirited tunes that add to the festive atmosphere. Here are some elements of beer hall music in Munich:

Oompah Bands: These are brass bands that often include trumpets, trombones, tubas, clarinets, and percussion instruments. They play a mix of traditional Bavarian music, polkas, marches, and popular tunes, creating a dynamic and engaging sound.

Folk Songs: Beer hall music often includes well-known folk songs, including "Ein Prosit," a popular German drinking song that is a staple during toasts at Oktoberfest and other beer-centric events.

Lively Atmosphere: The music in beer halls is meant to create a lively and celebratory ambiance. The tempo is often upbeat, encouraging dancing, singing along, and clapping to the rhythm.

Traditional Instruments: In addition to brass instruments, traditional Bavarian folk music might also include the accordion, fiddles, and sometimes yodeling, adding to the authentic and festive vibe.

Audience Participation: Beer hall music is often interactive, encouraging audience participation through sing-alongs, clapping, and even traditional dances like the Schuhplattler, a Bavarian folk dance.

Variety and Entertainment: While traditional Bavarian music dominates, you might also hear contemporary tunes or covers of popular songs, ensuring a mix of entertainment for all attendees.

Cultural Experience: Beer hall music offers visitors a glimpse into Bavarian culture, fostering a sense of community and celebration that is an integral part of the beer hall experience in Munich.

Whether it is the infectious melodies of brass bands, the communal singing of traditional songs, or the overall conviviality, beer hall music contributes significantly to the festive and vibrant atmosphere found in Munich's beer halls and during events like Oktoberfest.

Reinheitsgebot – German Pure Beer Laws, a Brief History

The history of German beer laws, famously known as Reinheitsgebot, traces back to a pivotal moment in Bavarian history.

In 1516, Duke Wilhelm IV and Duke Ludwig X of Bavaria issued what would become one of the world's oldest food purity regulations. The original text, known as the "Reinheitsgebot," decreed that beer could only be brewed using three ingredients: water, barley, and hops. This law aimed to protect consumers from unscrupulous brewers and ensure the quality of the beer.

Barley was mandated as the primary grain due to its suitability for brewing, while hops, known for their preservative properties and aromatic qualities, were added for flavor and stability. The use of water from pure sources was essential to prevent contamination.

Originally, this law was intended to regulate beer prices and maintain the quality of ingredients. Over time, it became a symbol of German beer culture and tradition. Brewers who wished to sell their beer in Bavaria had to comply with Reinheitsgebot, and variations of these regulations spread across different regions of Germany.

The law underwent several revisions and expansions, including allowing yeast as a permissible ingredient after its role in fermentation was discovered. These changes were made while still adhering to the core principles of purity and quality.

Reinheitsgebot's influence extended beyond Germany's borders. It became a benchmark for brewing standards, influencing brewing practices worldwide. Many breweries adopted similar principles even in regions without mandated purity laws, recognizing the value of simplicity and quality in brewing.

Despite its historical significance and cultural impact, Reinheitsgebot has faced criticism and challenges in the modern brewing landscape. Some argue that the law limits innovation and creativity in brewing by restricting the use of various ingredients and techniques that could enhance flavor profiles.

However, many traditional German breweries continue to uphold Reinheitsgebot, considering it a badge of honor and a testament to their commitment to producing high-quality, pure beer.

The legacy of Reinheitsgebot endures, embodying the rich history and traditions of German brewing while sparking ongoing debates about tradition, innovation, and the evolving nature of beer culture in a globalized world.

Oktoberfest

Oktoberfest, one of the world's largest and most famous folk festivals, traces its roots back to a royal wedding celebration in Munich.

The inaugural Oktoberfest took place in 1810 when Crown Prince Ludwig of Bavaria married Princess Therese of Saxony-Hildburghausen. The citizens of Munich were invited to join in the festivities held on fields outside the city gates, now known as Theresienwiese or "Wiesn" in honor of the princess. The celebration culminated with horse races, feasting, and beer-drinking.

Over time, Oktoberfest evolved into an annual event, gradually extending the duration, and diversifying its attractions. While the horse races eventually ceased, beer tents and amusement rides became central to the festival's identity.

The beer aspect became integral, with breweries setting up massive beer tents, each highlighting their brews. Traditional Bavarian music, vibrant folk costumes, and a jovial atmosphere characterized by Gemütlichkeit (coziness and sociability) became hallmarks of the festival.

Today, Oktoberfest spans 16–18 days, typically starting in late September and running into the first weekend of October. It attracts millions of visitors from around the world to Munich, transforming the city into a lively celebration of Bavarian culture.

The festival officially commences with the tapping of the first keg by Munich's mayor, who shouts "O'zapft is!" ("It's tapped!"). This marks the beginning of the beer consumption, and the festivities continue with parades, traditional Bavarian food, live music, and carnival attractions.

Each year, approximately six major Munich breweries, known as the "Big Six" (Hofbräu, Löwenbräu, Paulaner, Hacker-Pschorr, Spaten, and Augustiner), participate, serving their specially brewed Oktoberfestbier, a stronger and slightly darker version of traditional German lager.

The beer tents, ranging from large, iconic structures to smaller, more intimate ones, accommodate thousands of revelers, fostering an inclusive and joyous atmosphere. Patrons enjoy steins of beer, feast on hearty Bavarian delicacies like pretzels, sausages, and roasted chicken, and immerse themselves in traditional music and dancing.

Despite occasional interruptions due to wars and crises, Oktoberfest has persisted, adapting to modern times while preserving its cultural essence. The festival continues to evolve, incorporating modern entertainment while staying true to its centuries-old traditions, attracting beer enthusiasts, culture seekers, and revelers from across the globe to experience the unparalleled celebration of Bavarian heritage and Gemütlichkeit.

Famous Bavarian Beer Halls and Restaurants

Munich, the heartland of Bavarian beer culture, boasts several iconic beer halls, each with its unique charm, history, and vibrant atmosphere. Here are some of the most famous ones:

Hofbräuhaus: Arguably the most renowned beer hall globally, Hofbräuhaus traces its origins back to 1589. Founded by Duke Wilhelm V, this historic hall embodies Bavarian tradition. With its cavernous halls adorned with wooden tables, live music, and jovial atmosphere, it attracts locals and tourists alike. The flagship beer, Hofbräu, flows freely, and the hearty Bavarian dishes complement the beer-drinking experience. **Address: Platzl 9, 80331 München, Germany.**

Augustiner Bräustuben: Augustiner Brewery, one of Munich's oldest breweries dating back to 1328, offers a more intimate beer hall experience at its Bräustuben. Located near the main train station, this beer hall maintains a cozy, rustic ambiance. Augustiner's beers, known for their quality and authenticity, are served in traditional steins, and the menu features classic Bavarian cuisine. **Address: Landsberger Str. 19, 80339 München, Germany.**

Paulaner Bräuhaus: The Paulaner brewery's Bräuhaus provides a modern take on the traditional beer hall. Located in the heart of Munich, it offers a lively atmosphere, combining contemporary décor with nods to Bavarian heritage. Visitors can enjoy a diverse selection of Paulaner beers on tap while savoring hearty Bavarian dishes. **Address: Kapuzinerpl. 5, 80337 München, Germany.**

Löwenbräukeller: Founded in 1883 by the Löwenbräu brewery, Löwenbräukeller stands as a spacious beer hall with a beer garden that can accommodate large crowds. It exudes a festive ambiance, especially during Oktoberfest, with live music and an extensive beer selection, including their flagship Löwenbräu beer. **Address: Stiglmaierplatz, Nymphenburger Str. 2, 80335 München, Germany.**

Hacker-Pschorr Bräuhaus: This beer hall, located near Marienplatz, captures the essence of Bavarian conviviality. The Hacker-Pschorr beers, served here in traditional steins, accompany hearty Bavarian fare. The hall's historic architecture and bustling atmosphere create an authentic beer-drinking experience. **Address: Theresienhöhe 7 80339 Munich Germany.**

Andechser am Dom: While not as massive as some others, Andechser am Dom offers a cozy and traditional ambiance. Situated near Munich's famous Frauenkirche, it serves Andechs brewery's renowned beers, including their popular Doppelbock. The hall provides a quieter, more relaxed setting to enjoy Bavarian specialties and exceptional beer. **Address: Frauenplatz 7, 80331 München, Germany.**

These beer halls embody Munich's rich brewing heritage and vibrant social culture. Whether you are drawn to the historic ambiance of Hofbräuhaus or the cozy intimacy of smaller halls, each offers an authentic taste of Bavarian beer culture, fostering camaraderie, music, and of course, excellent beer.

Schneider Bräuhaus

Schneider Bräuhaus is a traditional Bavarian brewery and restaurant located in Munich. This establishment is known for its authentic Bavarian beer and food. Schneider Bräuhaus is not to be confused with the Schneider Weisse brewery, which is a separate brewery known for its wheat beers.

The Schneider Bräuhaus offers a cozy and welcoming atmosphere where visitors can enjoy a variety of traditional Bavarian dishes such as schnitzel, roast pork, pretzels, and more, paired with their locally brewed beer. It is a popular spot for both locals and tourists looking for an authentic Bavarian beer hall experience in Munich.

The brewery typically produces a range of Bavarian-style beers, including Helles, Dunkel, and Weißbier (wheat beer). The ambiance, hearty food, and quality beer make Schneider Bräuhaus a favorite destination for those seeking a genuine taste of Bavarian culture in Munich. **Address: Tal 7, 80331 München, Germany.**

Augustiner Klosterwirt

The Augustiner Klosterwirt offers a classic Bavarian beer hall experience where visitors can enjoy a range of Augustiner beers, including Helles (pale lager), Dunkel (dark lager), and Weißbier (wheat beer), among others. The atmosphere is typically warm and inviting, embodying the essence of Bavarian hospitality.

In addition to their excellent beers, the Augustiner Klosterwirt serves traditional Bavarian cuisine, including hearty dishes like roast pork (Schweinshaxe), sausages, pretzels, and other local specialties. It is a popular spot for locals and tourists alike, seeking an authentic taste of Bavarian beer culture in a historic setting.

The beer hall's ambiance, paired with delicious food and the renowned Augustiner beer, makes the Augustiner Klosterwirt a must-visit destination for anyone exploring Munich and wanting to experience the city's rich brewing heritage.
Address: Augustinerstraße 1, 80331 München, Germany.

Weihenstephan Brewery

Weihenstephan Brewery is not located in Munich, but rather in Freising, Bavaria, Germany, a short distance from Munich. It holds the title of the world's oldest continuously operating brewery, tracing its origins back to the Weihenstephan Abbey, which was founded in 725.

Weihenstephaner is celebrated for its longstanding brewing tradition, producing a range of exceptional beers. While not located directly in Munich, its beers are widely available and highly regarded not just in Bavaria but around the world.

Some of the popular beer styles produced by Weihenstephaner include:

Weißbier (Wheat Beer): Their Hefeweissbier and Kristallweissbier are acclaimed wheat beer varieties, known for their refreshing taste and distinctive flavors.

Lagers: Weihenstephaner also brews various lagers such as Helles, Pilsner, and Dunkel, maintaining the high quality and tradition that the brewery is renowned for.

Bock and Doppelbock: They produce strong and flavorful Bock beers, including their renowned Korbinian Doppelbock, which is rich and malty.

The brewery also collaborates with other breweries and institutions for research and development, contributing to innovations in brewing practices.

While Weihenstephaner Brewery is not situated in Munich itself, its beers are an integral part of Bavaria's brewing heritage and are often enjoyed in Munich's beer gardens, restaurants, and pubs, highlighting the region's rich beer culture.
Address: Weihenstephaner Berg 10, 85354 Freising, Germany.

Ayinger am Platzl

Ayinger am Platzl is a traditional Bavarian restaurant located in Munich, Germany. It is an establishment associated with the Ayinger Brewery, known for its longstanding brewing traditions and quality beers.

Ayinger am Platzl offers a cozy and authentic Bavarian atmosphere where visitors can experience traditional Bavarian cuisine and, of course, enjoy a selection of Ayinger's beers. The restaurant typically serves classic Bavarian dishes like schnitzel, roast pork, sausages, pretzels, and more, providing a genuine taste of Bavarian culinary culture.

Ayinger Brewery, while not directly attached to the restaurant, is highly esteemed for its range of beers, including their Bavarian-style lagers, wheat beers, and specialty brews. The beers are often available at Ayinger am Platzl, providing guests with the opportunity to pair their meal with excellent local brews.

The restaurant's location in Munich's historic center, along with its traditional ambiance and quality food and beer offerings, makes Ayinger am Platzl a popular spot for locals and tourists seeking an authentic Bavarian dining experience. **Address: Platzl 1A, 80331 München, Germany.**

Zum Franziskaner

"Zum Franziskaner" is a well-known and historic beer hall located in Munich, Germany. It is situated in the heart of the city, close to Marienplatz, and is celebrated for its traditional Bavarian atmosphere and cuisine.

The beer hall offers a quintessential Bavarian experience, serving a variety of traditional dishes such as roast pork, sausages, pretzels, and other local specialties. Visitors to Zum Franziskaner can enjoy classic Bavarian comfort food alongside a selection of quality beers, including Bavarian lagers, wheat beers, and more.The establishment's name translates to "At the Franciscan," and it has a long history dating back to the 14th century. Over the years, it has retained its charm and authenticity, making it a popular destination for both locals and tourists looking to immerse themselves in Munich's rich beer culture and enjoy hearty Bavarian cuisine.

Zum Franziskaner's central location, historic ambiance, and reputation for traditional Bavarian fare and beverages contribute to its appeal as a must-visit spot for those exploring Munich and seeking an authentic beer hall experience.
Address: Residenzstraße 9, 80333 München, Germany.

Ratskeller

The Ratskeller in Munich, Germany, is a historic beer hall and restaurant located in the basement of Munich's New Town Hall (Neues Rathaus) at Marienplatz. "Ratskeller" translates to "council's cellar," indicating its historical association with the city council.

This establishment is renowned for its traditional Bavarian ambiance and cuisine, offering visitors a taste of classic Bavarian dishes in a historic setting. The Ratskeller serves a variety of hearty meals such as roast pork, sausages, dumplings, and pretzels, accompanied by a selection of Bavarian beers and wines.

The Ratskeller's architecture and décor reflect a mix of Gothic and Renaissance styles, providing a unique and charming atmosphere for dining and enjoying Bavarian specialties. The establishment also houses one of the most extensive wine cellars in Germany, offering a diverse selection of wines.

With its central location in the heart of Munich's historic Marienplatz and its historic significance as part of the New Town Hall, the Ratskeller remains a popular destination for locals and tourists alike seeking an authentic Bavarian dining experience in a historically rich setting. **Address: Marienplatz 8, 80331 München, Germany.**

Paulaner im Tal

This establishment is part of the Paulaner brewery tradition, offering a typical Bavarian dining experience.

At Paulaner im Tal, visitors can enjoy a variety of Bavarian specialties, including traditional dishes such as roast pork, schnitzel, sausages, pretzels, and other regional delicacies. The restaurant serves these hearty meals alongside a selection of Paulaner beers, known for their quality and adherence to Bavarian brewing traditions.

The venue often provides both indoor dining spaces in a cozy Bavarian-style setting and an outdoor beer garden during warmer months. This allows guests to savor their meals and beers in a lively and convivial atmosphere.

Paulaner im Tal's central location in Munich, combined with its reputation for serving authentic Bavarian cuisine and offering a taste of Paulaner's renowned beers, makes it a favored destination for both locals and tourists seeking an authentic Bavarian dining experience in the heart of Munich.
Address: Tal 12, 80331 München, Germany.

Hofbräuhaus

The Hofbräuhaus in Munich, Germany, is one of the world's most famous beer halls and a landmark of

Bavarian culture. Established in 1589 by the Duke of Bavaria, it has a rich history and remains a significant symbol of Munich's beer culture.

The Hofbräuhaus offers visitors an authentic Bavarian beer hall experience. The massive hall features communal tables, lively music from traditional bands, and an atmosphere that embodies the spirit of Bavarian conviviality.

Patrons can enjoy a variety of traditional Bavarian dishes such as roast pork, sausages, pretzels, and other specialties, paired with Hofbräu beer, known for its quality and distinct taste. The beer served here includes classics like Helles (pale lager), Dunkel (dark lager), and Weißbier (wheat beer).

The beer hall's ambiance, combined with its rich history and cultural significance, attracts both locals and tourists. It is a must-visit destination for those seeking an authentic Bavarian beer hall experience in Munich. The Hofbräuhaus continues to uphold its tradition while welcoming guests from around the world to revel in Bavarian hospitality.
Address: Platzl 9, 80331 München, Germany.

Hofbräukeller

The Hofbräukeller in Munich, Germany, is a historic beer garden and restaurant nestled in the Haidhausen district. Established in 1892, this traditional Bavarian establishment is an integral part of Munich's beer culture and heritage.

The Hofbräukeller offers a quintessential Bavarian experience, featuring a spacious beer garden where patrons can relax under chestnut trees while enjoying a selection of Bavarian beers, including classic varieties like Helles, Dunkel, and Weißbier.

Visitors to the Hofbräukeller can savor a range of traditional Bavarian dishes such as roast pork, sausages, pretzels, and other regional specialties. The ambiance exudes a cozy and welcoming atmosphere, with a mix of indoor and outdoor seating, live music, and a convivial atmosphere, especially during warmer months.

With its historic roots and commitment to Bavarian traditions, the Hofbräukeller remains a popular destination for locals and tourists seeking an authentic beer garden experience in Munich. It is an ideal spot to enjoy hearty Bavarian fare, quality beers, and soak in the vibrant atmosphere that embodies the essence of Bavarian hospitality. **Address: Innere Wiener Straße 19, 81667 München, Germany.**

Brewery Tours in Munich

In Munich, Germany, brewery tours offer an immersive experience into the city's rich beer culture and brewing traditions. Some renowned breweries in Munich and its vicinity offer guided tours that allow visitors to explore the brewing process, history, and tasting sessions. Here are a few breweries known for their tours:

Hofbräuhaus: The iconic Hofbräuhaus in Munich conducts brewery tours that offer insights into its brewing techniques and history. Visitors can learn about the brewing process and enjoy a tasting session of Hofbräu beers.

Paulaner Brewery: The Paulaner Brewery provides guided tours that take visitors through their brewing facilities, highlighting the beer-making process. The tour often ends with a tasting session of their classic Bavarian brews.

Augustiner Brewery: While not directly in Munich city, the Augustiner Brewery in Munich's outskirts (in Neuhaus) offers tours that delve into the brewery's history and brewing methods. Visitors can enjoy guided tours followed by a tasting of their renowned beers.

Weihenstephan Brewery: Though located a short distance from Munich in Freising, the Weihenstephan Brewery, being the world's oldest brewery, offers fascinating tours exploring its brewing traditions, history, and modern production techniques.

Private and Group Tours: Additionally, some tour companies in Munich organize brewery tours, allowing participants to visit multiple breweries, learn about the brewing process, and enjoy tastings while providing transportation and expert guidance.

It is recommended to check the breweries' websites or contact them directly for tour availability, schedules, and booking details, as they might have specific timings and requirements for reservations. Brewery tours in Munich offer a fantastic opportunity to learn about the city's beer heritage and enjoy tastings of Bavaria's renowned brews.

Hofbräu Beer

Hofbräuhaus, one of the most iconic breweries in the world, has a history deeply rooted in Bavarian tradition and royalty.

Founded in 1589 by Duke Wilhelm V of Bavaria, Hofbräuhaus originally served as a royal brewery exclusively for the Duke's court in Munich. The brewery's name, "Hofbräu," translates to "court brewery," reflecting its noble origins.

Initially, Hofbräuhaus brewed beer for the Duke's own enjoyment, crafted under strict quality standards. Its reputation for excellence soon spread beyond the palace walls, and in 1607, Hofbräuhaus opened its doors to the public, making its exceptional beer available to the citizens of Munich.

Over the centuries, Hofbräuhaus became a focal point of Bavarian culture, drawing locals and visitors alike to its massive beer halls filled with lively music, hearty food, and, of course, the renowned Hofbräu beer. Its fame transcended borders, attracting tourists from around the globe who sought an authentic taste of Bavarian brewing tradition.

The brewery faced challenges throughout history, including damage during wars and changes in ownership. However, it persevered, rebuilding and expanding its operations to meet the growing demand for its distinctive brews.

One of Hofbräuhaus's most significant moments occurred in the 19th century when King Ludwig I of Bavaria decided to sell beer brewed at Hofbräuhaus outside Munich. This decision expanded the brewery's reach, establishing Hofbräuhaus as an internationally recognized brand.

Today, Hofbräuhaus continues to thrive as a symbol of Bavarian hospitality and beer culture. Its flagship beer, Hofbräu Original, remains a favorite, characterized by its golden color, balanced flavor, and a slightly hoppy aroma. The brewery also produces a range of other beer styles, catering to diverse tastes.

Hofbräuhaus in Munich stands as a bustling institution, welcoming visitors to experience the authentic atmosphere of a traditional Bavarian beer hall. Its history, intertwined with Bavaria's royal legacy and a commitment to brewing excellence, has cemented its place in the pantheon of iconic breweries worldwide.

Paulaner Beer

Paulaner Brewery, one of Munich's oldest and most esteemed breweries, has a history that intertwines tradition, innovation, and a commitment to quality beer craftsmanship.

The origins of Paulaner date back to the 17th century when it was established by the Paulaner monks in the Cloister Neudeck ob der Au in Munich. The monastery initially brewed beer to support its activities and aid charitable causes. The monks' dedication to brewing excellence laid the foundation for what would become a renowned brewery.

In 1634, during the Thirty Years' War, the monks crafted a special strong beer known as "Salvator" to commemorate their founder, Saint Francis of Paola. Salvator, with its rich maltiness and higher alcohol content, became an annual tradition and the flagship beer of Paulaner.

As brewing technology advanced, Paulaner grew beyond its monastic origins. In 1799, after secularization led to the dissolution of the monasteries, the brewery was acquired by Franz Xaver Zacherl, marking the beginning of its commercial expansion.

Over the years, Paulaner continued to innovate while staying true to its brewing heritage. It became one of the six breweries involved in the inaugural Oktoberfest celebration in 1810, solidifying its status as an integral part of Munich's beer culture.

In the late 19th and early 20th centuries, Paulaner underwent modernization, adopting new brewing techniques and expanding its range of beers. Despite challenges during World War I and World War II, the brewery persisted, contributing to Munich's post-war reconstruction and the revival of its beer industry.

Paulaner's commitment to tradition and quality never wavered. Its beers, including the iconic Salvator Doppelbock, remained a symbol of Bavarian brewing excellence. As the craft beer movement gained momentum, Paulaner continued to innovate, introducing new styles while preserving its classic recipes.

In 2015, Paulaner merged with Brau Holding International, uniting with other renowned breweries. This consolidation aimed to strengthen its position in the global beer market while maintaining its dedication to traditional brewing methods.

Today, Paulaner Brewery stands as a pillar of Bavarian brewing tradition. It produces a diverse range of beers, from classic lagers to specialty brews, all brewed with the same commitment to quality and heritage that has defined the brand for centuries. Its presence extends beyond Munich, making Paulaner beers cherished by beer enthusiasts worldwide.

Spaten Brewery

Spaten Brewery, one of Munich's oldest and most esteemed breweries, has a rich history steeped in Bavarian tradition and innovation.

The brewery was established in 1397 by Hans Welser, making it one of the city's oldest breweries. In 1807, the Spaten Brewery was acquired by Gabriel Sedlmayr, a member of the Sedlmayr family renowned for their contributions to Bavarian brewing.

Under the leadership of Gabriel Sedlmayr and later his son, Joseph Sedlmayr, Spaten underwent significant advancements in brewing technology and techniques. The Sedlmayrs were pioneers in introducing English-style brewing methods, notably the use of bottom-fermenting yeast and refrigeration, which revolutionized beer production.

In 1841, Spaten Brewery played a pivotal role in developing the Märzen style of beer, a malty lager brewed in March (März in German) and traditionally consumed during Oktoberfest. This innovation solidified Spaten's reputation as a leading brewery in Bavaria.

Throughout the 19th and 20th centuries, Spaten Brewery continued to flourish, earning recognition for its commitment to quality and innovation. Its beers, including the renowned Spaten München Lager and Spaten Optimator Doppelbock, gained popularity not only in Munich but also internationally.

In 1922, Spaten merged with Franziskaner-Leist Bräu, another prominent Munich brewery, forming the Spaten-Franziskaner-Bräu. This merger further strengthened Spaten's position in the beer market and expanded its range of offerings.

Over the years, Spaten Brewery remained dedicated to its traditional brewing methods while adapting to modern standards. In 1997, Spaten-Franziskaner-Bräu became part of the global brewing conglomerate, InBev, which later merged with Anheuser-Busch to form Anheuser-Busch InBev (AB InBev), one of the world's largest brewing companies.

Despite these changes in ownership, Spaten's commitment to brewing high-quality, classic Bavarian beers persisted. Its beers continue to be brewed according to traditional recipes, adhering to the standards set forth by the Reinheitsgebot (German Beer Purity Law).

Today, Spaten Brewery remains a symbol of Munich's brewing heritage and a key player in Bavaria's beer culture. Its classic brews and contributions to beer styles have left an indelible mark on the global beer landscape, embodying centuries of Bavarian brewing excellence.

Augustiner Brewery

Augustiner Brewery holds a distinguished place in Munich's brewing history, renowned for its rich tradition, quality beers, and emphasis on Bavarian authenticity.

Founded in 1328 by Augustinian monks, Augustiner Brewery has an illustrious past, starting as a monastery brewery within the Augustinian order. The monks brewed beer as a means of sustenance and to support charitable causes. Their commitment to brewing excellence and adherence to traditional methods laid the foundation for Augustiner's esteemed reputation.

Despite the secularization that led to the dissolution of many monasteries, Augustiner Brewery persisted, transitioning into a secular brewery. Over the centuries, it maintained its dedication to brewing high-quality beers while staying true to its Bavarian roots.

Augustiner's commitment to tradition is exemplified by its adherence to old-fashioned brewing techniques, including the use of wooden barrels for fermentation and storage, which contribute to the unique character of its beers.

One of its most iconic brews is the Augustiner Helles, a pale lager known for its balanced maltiness, gentle hop character, and smooth, crisp finish. Augustiner's beers, including its Edelstoff and Maximator Doppelbock, have gained admiration for their consistency and adherence to Reinheitsgebot, the German Beer Purity Law.

The brewery's beer halls, such as the Augustiner Bräustuben near the main train station and the Augustiner-Keller beer garden, provide an authentic Bavarian beer-drinking experience. These venues exude a cozy, traditional ambiance, offering a welcoming atmosphere for locals and visitors alike to enjoy their brews alongside classic Bavarian cuisine.

Augustiner Brewery operates as a private, independent brewery, distinguishing itself from larger conglomerates. This independence allows it to maintain its focus on quality over quantity and to preserve its cherished brewing heritage.

In Munich's dynamic beer landscape, Augustiner Brewery stands as a testament to the enduring allure of tradition and craftsmanship. Its commitment to producing exceptional beers while upholding centuries-old brewing techniques has solidified its place as a beloved institution in Bavaria's vibrant beer culture.

Löwenbräu Brewery

Löwenbräu Brewery, with its longstanding history and iconic lion emblem, is an integral part of

Munich's illustrious brewing heritage.

Founded in 1383 by the Lyon family, Löwenbräu, translating to "lion's brew," derived its name from the lion, a symbol of strength and nobility. Initially, the brewery was located outside Munich's city walls to avoid city taxes, but its reputation for quality beer soon drew attention within the city.

By the 19th century, Löwenbräu had gained prominence and moved its operations to a larger facility within Munich. This expansion facilitated increased production and distribution of its renowned beers, laying the foundation for its global recognition.

Löwenbräu's flagship beer, Löwenbräu Original, is a traditional Bavarian helles lager characterized by its golden color, balanced malt sweetness, and mild hop bitterness. It has become synonymous with the brewery's commitment to brewing excellence and adherence to Bavarian brewing traditions.

The brewery's iconic lion logo adorns its beer labels, signifying the brand's legacy and strength in the competitive brewing landscape. Over the years, Löwenbräu has maintained its dedication to quality, consistently delivering beers that reflect the essence of Bavarian brewing.

The Löwenbräu beer hall, located near the city center, offers a quintessential Bavarian beer experience. Its lively ambiance, traditional décor, and hearty Bavarian cuisine create an authentic setting for enjoying Löwenbräu's brews in the heart of Munich.

In the late 20th century, Löwenbräu became part of larger brewing conglomerates, contributing to its expanded reach across global markets. However, despite changes in ownership, the brewery has retained its commitment to brewing traditional beers and upholding its Bavarian heritage.

Today, Löwenbräu Brewery remains a prominent figure in Munich's beer culture. Its enduring legacy, symbolized by the proud lion, continues to resonate with beer enthusiasts worldwide, highlighting the enduring appeal of Bavarian brewing traditions and quality craftsmanship.

Hacker-Pschorr Brewery

Hacker-Pschorr Brewery, deeply rooted in Bavarian brewing history, stands as a testament to tradition, quality, and innovation in Munich's beer culture.

The brewery's origins trace back to the 15th century when the Hacker and Pschorr families separately began brewing in Munich. Over time, the two families' breweries grew in prominence, and in 1972, they officially merged to form Hacker-Pschorr, combining their brewing expertise and heritage.

Hacker-Pschorr Brewery's commitment to excellence and adherence to Bavarian brewing traditions earned it a distinguished reputation. The brewery's beers are crafted following the principles of Reinheitsgebot, the German Beer Purity Law, using only high-quality ingredients.

Among its renowned brews, the Hacker-Pschorr Oktoberfest Märzen holds a special place. This amber-hued lager, characterized by its rich maltiness, balanced hops, and smooth finish, became an integral part of Munich's Oktoberfest celebration, where it is served in large quantities.

The brewery's commitment to innovation while preserving tradition is evident in its diverse range of beers. From classic helles lagers to darker bocks and wheat beers, Hacker-Pschorr offers a variety of styles that cater to diverse palates.

Hacker-Pschorr's beer hall, the Pschorr Bräurosl, located on the Oktoberfest grounds, provides a vibrant and authentic Bavarian beer experience. The hall's festive atmosphere, traditional music, and hearty Bavarian dishes complement the brewery's exceptional beers.

Throughout its history, Hacker-Pschorr has navigated changes in ownership while maintaining its dedication to brewing top-quality beers. The brewery's enduring legacy, marked by its distinct lion logo and commitment to tradition, continues to resonate with beer enthusiasts both in Munich and around the world.

As part of the larger beer conglomerate, Paulaner Brauerei Group, Hacker-Pschorr remains a key player in preserving Bavarian brewing traditions, highlighting its heritage, and delivering exceptional beers that honor centuries of brewing excellence.

Andechser am Dom

Andechser am Dom represents a unique blend of tradition, spirituality, and exceptional beer craftsmanship in Munich's brewing landscape.

The history of Andechser am Dom is intertwined with the Andechs Monastery, located outside Munich. This Benedictine monastery has a centuries-old brewing tradition that dates to the Middle Ages. The monks brewed beer both for sustenance within the monastery and to support charitable causes.

The Andechs Monastery's brewing legacy gained recognition for its commitment to quality, adhering to traditional brewing methods and using natural ingredients. This dedication to excellence has transcended time and remains a hallmark of Andechser am Dom's beers.

Andechser am Dom's beer hall, situated near Munich's famous Frauenkirche (Cathedral of Our Dear Lady), provides a serene and intimate setting, offering a departure from the bustling crowds of larger beer halls. The venue reflects a sense of tranquility and spiritual heritage while serving exceptional Bavarian beers crafted by the Andechs Monastery.

The brewery's beers, including their celebrated Doppelbock and Helles Lager, embody the monastery's brewing traditions. These beers are characterized by their rich flavors, balanced profiles, and adherence to Reinheitsgebot, the German Beer Purity Law, using only water, malt, hops, and yeast.

Andechser am Dom's commitment to sustainability and environmental responsibility is also evident in its brewing practices. The brewery emphasizes eco-friendly initiatives and strives to maintain a harmonious relationship with nature, aligning with the Benedictine values of stewardship and respect for the environment.

While Andechser am Dom may not boast the size or grandeur of larger beer halls, its focus on quality, heritage, and spiritual connection sets it apart. Visitors to this intimate beer hall experience a taste of Bavarian tradition, coupled with a sense of reverence for the monastery's centuries-old brewing legacy.

Schneider Weisse

Schneider Weisse, a Bavarian brewery renowned for its exceptional wheat beers, has a history steeped in tradition and innovation, highlighting a commitment to quality and craftsmanship.

The brewery's origins trace back to 1872 when Georg Schneider I purchased the Weisses Brauhaus, a brewery founded in the 19th century. Georg Schneider I had a vision to specialize in wheat beer production, a style traditionally associated with Bavaria but less prevalent at that time.

Georg Schneider I's foresight led to the revival of wheat beer brewing in Bavaria, a style that had diminished in popularity due to changes in tastes and brewing regulations. His dedication to brewing exclusively wheat beers, particularly the darker, stronger version known as "Weizenbock," earned Schneider Weisse a distinctive place in the beer landscape.

One of Schneider Weisse's iconic brews is the Schneider Weisse Original, a classic wheat beer appreciated for its cloudy appearance, rich yeast character, and balanced flavors of banana and clove. The brewery also produces a variety of wheat beers, including Aventinus Eisbock and Tap 7 Unser Original.

Schneider Weisse's commitment to tradition is evident in its adherence to traditional brewing methods, using open fermentation and bottle-conditioning to develop the beer's distinctive flavors and aromas.

The brewery's dedication to quality extends beyond its brewing processes. Schneider Weisse focuses on sustainability and environmental responsibility, embracing eco-friendly practices in its operations.

While Schneider Weisse may not operate a large-scale beer hall like some of Munich's famous breweries, its beers are revered among enthusiasts for their authenticity and craftsmanship. The brewery's presence in Munich and its global reach exemplifies the enduring legacy of Georg Schneider I's vision and the continued appreciation for Bavarian wheat beers.

Klosterbrauerei Andechs

Klosterbrauerei Andechs, nestled in the Bavarian Alps, represents a unique combination of spirituality, heritage, and exceptional brewing craftsmanship, making it a revered institution in Germany's beer culture.

The brewery's story begins within the Andechs Monastery, a Benedictine abbey founded in the 9th century. For centuries, monks at Andechs brewed beer as part of their monastic traditions. This brewing legacy evolved over time, becoming an integral aspect of the monastery's cultural and charitable contributions.

Andechs' brewing heritage gained recognition for its commitment to quality and adherence to traditional brewing techniques. The brewery's location atop the "Holy Mountain" contributes to the pure, pristine water source used in brewing, a crucial element in producing exceptional beers.

Andechs offers a range of beers, each crafted with precision and care. Its Doppelbock stands as a flagship brew, known for its rich maltiness, robust character, and smooth finish. The brewery also produces various traditional Bavarian beer styles, including Helles Lager and Weissbier, each reflecting the monastery's dedication to brewing excellence.

Klosterbrauerei Andechs operates a beer hall and beer garden adjacent to the monastery, providing visitors with an authentic Bavarian beer experience. The venue exudes a serene yet convivial ambiance, offering a setting where patrons can savor Andechs' finely crafted brews amidst the monastery's picturesque surroundings.

Beyond its commitment to brewing exceptional beers, Andechs places great emphasis on sustainability and environmental stewardship. The brewery implements eco-friendly practices, aligning with the Benedictine values of respect for nature and responsible stewardship of resources.

Klosterbrauerei Andechs' enduring legacy embodies a harmonious blend of tradition, spirituality, and brewing expertise. Its commitment to quality, heritage, and sustainability resonates with beer enthusiasts, fostering a deep appreciation for Bavarian brewing traditions and the monastery's rich cultural heritage. **Address: Bergstraße 2, 82346 Andechs, Germany.**

Getting there via S-Bahn: The S8 leaves every 20 minutes and takes 50 minutes. It is the last stop on this S-Bahn line, called Herrsching. After you arrive at Herrsching, you will begin your walk up the mountain. There is an easy-to-read trail map right after the train station, or you can just follow the signs pointing to where to go.

Munich Lodging and Accommodations

Munich offers a diverse range of lodging options that cater to various preferences and budgets. From luxury hotels to budget-friendly hostels and charming guesthouses, here is a snapshot of lodging in Munich:

Luxury Hotels: Munich boasts several high-end hotels known for their luxury amenities, impeccable service, and prime locations. These hotels often feature spa facilities, fine dining restaurants, and elegant rooms. Some renowned options include Bayerischer Hof, Hotel Vier Jahreszeiten Kempinski, and The Charles Hotel.

Mid-Range Hotels: There are numerous mid-range hotels in Munich that offer comfortable accommodations with modern amenities. They provide a balance between quality and affordability. Hotels like Maritim Hotel München, NH Collection München Bavaria, and Platzl Hotel Munich fall into this category.

Budget-Friendly Options: For travelers seeking more budget-friendly options, Munich has hostels and budget hotels that provide affordable stays without compromising on basic amenities. Wombats City Hostel, Euro Youth Hotel, and MEININGER Hotel Munich City Center are popular choices among budget-conscious travelers.

Guesthouses and Bed & Breakfasts: Munich also offers quaint guesthouses and bed & breakfast accommodations, providing a more personalized and homely experience. These often feature cozy rooms, local charm, and personalized service. Gästehaus Englischer Garten and Pension Seibel are examples of such accommodations.

Apartment Rentals: For those seeking a more independent stay, there is a growing availability of vacation rentals and serviced apartments in Munich. Platforms like Airbnb offer a variety of options, from private rooms to entire apartments, catering to different group sizes and preferences.

Location Considerations: The city center, Altstadt-Lehel, is a popular area to stay due to its proximity to attractions like Marienplatz and the historic center. Other districts like Maxvorstadt, Schwabing, and Glockenbachviertel offer a vibrant atmosphere with restaurants, bars, and cultural spots.

Overall, Munich provides a wide array of lodging choices, catering to the diverse needs of travelers, whether they seek luxury, budget-friendly options, or a more local and personalized experience. The choice of accommodation often depends on the traveler's preferences, the purpose of the visit, and desired proximity to specific attractions or areas within the city.

Dining and Meals in Munich

Dining in Munich offers a delightful blend of traditional Bavarian cuisine, international flavors, and diverse culinary experiences. Here is an overview of the dining scene in Munich:

Bavarian Cuisine: Munich is renowned for its authentic Bavarian dishes. From hearty classics like weißwurst (white sausage), schnitzel, pretzels, and sauerkraut to rich dishes like Schweinshaxe (pork knuckle) and hearty stews, local eateries serve up traditional Bavarian fare. Beer halls and taverns offer a quintessential experience, pairing these dishes with local brews.

Beer Gardens: Munich's beer gardens are iconic social hubs where locals and tourists gather to enjoy fresh brews and traditional dishes amidst a lively atmosphere. Places like Hofbräuhaus, Augustiner-Keller, and Englischer Garten's beer garden offer an authentic Bavarian experience.

International Cuisine: Munich's dining scene reflects its cosmopolitan nature. The city hosts a variety of international cuisines, including Italian, Asian, Middle Eastern, and more. Trendy neighborhoods like Schwabing and Glockenbachviertel feature diverse restaurants, bistros, and cafes offering international flavors.

Fine Dining: Munich boasts numerous Michelin-starred restaurants and upscale dining establishments catering to discerning palates. These venues offer exquisite dishes crafted with innovative techniques and premium ingredients. Places like Tantris and Dallmayr display high-end culinary experiences.

Markets and Food Halls: Munich's food markets like Viktualienmarkt offer a vibrant mix of fresh produce, local specialties, and street food stalls. These markets are perfect for sampling regional delicacies, buying fresh ingredients, or enjoying a quick snack.

Cafés and Bakeries: Munich's café culture is thriving, with charming cafes and bakeries serving artisanal pastries, cakes, and coffee. Cafés like Café Frischhut and Aroma Kaffeebar are beloved spots for a relaxing break.

Vegetarian and Vegan Options: The city caters well to vegetarians and vegans, with an increasing number of restaurants offering plant-based menus and options.

Overall, Munich's dining scene is diverse and dynamic, highlighting a rich tapestry of flavors, from hearty traditional dishes to innovative culinary creations. Whether dining in cozy taverns, elegant restaurants, bustling markets, or quaint cafés, visitors can explore a variety of gastronomic delights while embracing Bavarian hospitality and culinary traditions.

Transportation in Munich

Getting around Munich is convenient and efficient thanks to its well-developed public transportation system and walkable city center. No rental car is needed. Here is a summary of travel options within Munich:

Public Transportation: Munich boasts an extensive and reliable public transportation network comprising the U-Bahn (subway), S-Bahn (urban trains), trams, and buses. The MVV (Munich Transport and Tariff Association) manages these services, offering various ticket options for different travel durations and zones.

U-Bahn and S-Bahn: The U-Bahn covers the city center and outer districts, while the S-Bahn connects Munich with suburban areas and neighboring towns. Both systems are punctual, making them ideal for navigating the city and reaching attractions efficiently.

Trams and Buses: Trams and buses supplement the U-Bahn and S-Bahn networks, providing additional coverage, especially to areas not directly serviced by trains. They are convenient for reaching specific neighborhoods and landmarks.

Biking: Munich is bike-friendly, offering dedicated bike lanes and rental services. Exploring the city on a bike is a popular option, especially in the warmer months. The city's flat terrain and bike-friendly infrastructure make it enjoyable for cyclists.

Walking: Munich's city center is relatively compact and easily walkable. Many attractions, such as Marienplatz, Viktualienmarkt, and Englischer Garten, are within walking distance of each other. Walking allows for a more intimate exploration of the city's charm and architecture.

Taxis and Ridesharing: Taxis are readily available in Munich and can be hailed on the street or booked through apps. Ridesharing services like Uber also operate in the city, providing additional transportation options.

Car Rentals: While Munich has an efficient public transit system, car rentals are available for travelers who prefer driving. However, parking in the city center can be limited and expensive, so using public transport might be more convenient.

Day Trips: Munich's central location makes it an excellent hub for day trips to nearby attractions such as Neuschwanstein Castle, Salzburg, Nuremberg, and the Bavarian Alps. Trains and buses connect Munich to these destinations, offering convenient options for day excursions.

Overall, Munich offers a variety of transportation modes, making it easy for visitors to explore the city and its surroundings. The well-connected public transit system, combined with walkable streets and biking options, allows travelers to navigate Munich comfortably while enjoying its cultural and historical treasures.

Getting to Munich

Traveling to Munich, Germany, offers a blend of rich history, Bavarian culture, stunning architecture, and a vibrant atmosphere. Here is a summary to guide your trip:

Arrival: Munich International Airport (Franz Josef Strauss Airport) serves as the primary gateway for international travelers. It is well-connected to the city center via efficient public transport, including S-Bahn trains and airport shuttles.

Accommodations: Munich offers a diverse range of lodging options, from luxury hotels to budget-friendly hostels and charming guesthouses. The city center, Altstadt-Lehel, is popular for its proximity to attractions, but other districts like Maxvorstadt and Schwabing also offer great options.

Sightseeing: Munich is a city rich in history and culture. Key attractions include Marienplatz with the Glockenspiel, Frauenkirche, Viktualienmarkt, Englischer Garten (one of the world's largest urban parks), and iconic beer halls like Hofbräuhaus.

Museums and Galleries: Munich boasts numerous world-class museums and galleries. The Alte Pinakothek, Neue Pinakothek, and Pinakothek der Moderne house impressive art collections. The

Deutsches Museum is Europe's largest science and technology museum.

Culinary Delights: Indulge in Bavarian cuisine at traditional beer halls and local taverns. Do not miss trying classic dishes like weißwurst, pretzels, schnitzel, and sampling the renowned Bavarian beer in beer gardens like Hofbräuhaus or Augustiner-Keller.

Day Trips: Munich's central location allows for easy day trips to attractions like Neuschwanstein Castle, the fairy-tale castle of King Ludwig II, the charming town of Nuremberg, or the picturesque landscapes of the Bavarian Alps.

Transportation: Munich has an efficient public transportation system comprising U-Bahn, S-Bahn, trams, and buses. The city is also walkable, allowing visitors to explore its beauty on foot or by bike. Taxis, ride-sharing services, and car rentals are readily available.

Events and Festivals: Munich hosts events throughout the year, including the world-famous Oktoberfest, Christmas markets, and cultural festivals celebrating music, art, and traditions.

Visiting Munich offers a captivating mix of history, culture, culinary delights, and picturesque landscapes. Whether exploring historic landmarks, indulging in Bavarian cuisine, or venturing on day trips, Munich promises an enriching and memorable experience.

Munich's U-Bahn and S-Bahn

Using the Munich subway, known as the U-Bahn/S-Bahn, is an efficient way to navigate the city. Here is a summary to guide you through using the Munich subway:

Understanding the System: The Munich U-Bahn/S-Bahn consists of several lines identified by numbers and colors on maps and signs. Each line connects various parts of the city, including key attractions, neighborhoods, and transportation hubs.

Tickets and Tariffs: Purchase tickets at vending machines located at U-Bahn/S-Bahn stations or via the MVV app. Ticket options vary based on the number of zones and duration. Validate tickets before boarding by stamping them at the blue machines on platforms.

Frequency and Schedule: Trains run frequently, especially during peak hours, with intervals of a few minutes. Operating hours typically range from around 4:30 AM until approximately 1:00 AM, though exact times can vary by line and day of the week.

Navigating Stations: Stations are well-marked and have clear signage indicating lines, directions, and connections. Platform screens and audio announcements provide information about upcoming trains, stops, and connections.

Boarding and Exiting: Wait behind the yellow line on platforms until the train arrives. Allow passengers to exit before boarding. Doors open automatically at stops, and it is courteous to let people disembark before entering.

Accessibility: U-Bahn/S-Bahn stations and trains are generally accessible to people with disabilities or mobility challenges. Many stations have elevators, escalators, and tactile guidance systems for visually impaired travelers.

Safety and Etiquette: Keep an eye on belongings, especially in crowded areas. It is customary to offer seats to the elderly, pregnant women, or people with disabilities. Avoid blocking doors during rush hours and maintain quiet in the train.

Connections: The U-Bahn/S-Bahn integrates with other public transport modes like trams and buses. Many stations also have bike parking facilities.

Navigating the Munich subway is straightforward and convenient, providing a reliable way to explore the city's attractions and neighborhoods while experiencing the efficiency of the city's public transportation system.

Munich Airport (MUC)

Munich Airport, officially known as Franz Josef Strauss Airport (MUC), stands as a modern and well-equipped international airport serving Munich and its surrounding regions. Here is an overview:

Facilities: MUC boasts modern facilities, including a wide array of shops, restaurants, lounges, and services spread across its terminals. These amenities cater to the needs of travelers, providing shopping opportunities, dining choices, and relaxation areas.

Terminals: The airport comprises two main terminals—Terminal 1 and Terminal 2—connected by the Munich Airport Center (MAC). Terminal 1 primarily serves Lufthansa, and its Star Alliance partners, while Terminal 2 handles other carriers. Both terminals offer efficient services for departures, arrivals, and transfers.

Transportation: Munich Airport is well-connected to the city center and surrounding areas. The S-Bahn (urban trains) S1 and S8 lines connect the airport to downtown Munich, providing a convenient and cost-effective means of transportation. Taxis, rental cars, and buses are also available for travel to various destinations.

Amenities: The airport features a range of amenities to enhance the travel experience, including lounges, children's play areas, prayer rooms, showers, and luggage storage facilities. Duty-free shopping, diverse dining options, and comfortable seating areas are available throughout the terminals.

Efficiency: Known for its efficiency and cleanliness, Munich Airport offers smooth and organized operations. Security checks and immigration processes are typically swift, contributing to a stress-free travel experience.

Services: MUC provides comprehensive services, including currency exchange, ATMs, medical facilities, Wi-Fi access, information desks, and assistance for passengers with reduced mobility or special needs.

Expansion and Innovation: The airport continually evolves with ongoing expansions and technological advancements. It prioritizes sustainability and environmental initiatives, striving to maintain a balance between growth and eco-friendly practices.

Business and Conferences: Munich Airport offers facilities for business travelers, including meeting rooms, conference spaces, and business lounges, catering to the needs of corporate travelers.

Munich Airport serves as a modern and traveler-friendly gateway to the city and beyond, offering a seamless travel experience with its range of amenities, efficient services, and well-connected transportation options.

Expenses in Munich

Touring Munich can involve various costs depending on your preferences, travel style, and activities. Here is an overview of typical expenses to consider:

Accommodation: Accommodation costs in Munich vary based on the type of lodging. Budget hostels or guesthouses can range from €20-€60 per night. Mid-range hotels may cost around €80-€150, while luxury hotels can exceed €200 per night.

Transportation: Munich's public transportation system is efficient and affordable. A single trip within the city costs around €2.90-€3.40. Day tickets or multi-day passes offer better value if you plan to use public transport frequently. A day ticket for the inner city (MVV Gesamtnetz) costs approximately €8.80.

Food and Dining: Dining costs vary widely. A meal at a casual restaurant might range from €10-€25 per person. Beer garden or traditional Bavarian meals can cost around €15-€30. Fine dining or Michelin-starred restaurants can be more expensive, ranging from €50-€100 or more per person.

Attractions and Activities: Many attractions in Munich offer free admission or have nominal entry fees. For instance, visiting public parks or

Marienplatz is free, while museum entry fees might range from €5-€15 per person.

Day Trips: If planning day trips to nearby attractions like Neuschwanstein Castle or Salzburg, consider additional costs for transportation, entrance fees, and guided tours. Prices for organized tours or transportation vary.

Shopping and Souvenirs: Munich offers various shopping opportunities, from local markets to designer boutiques. Prices for souvenirs, clothing, or specialty items can vary significantly.

Entertainment and Events: Costs for concerts, festivals, or special events in Munich vary. Entry fees for events like Oktoberfest or Christmas markets can range from nominal charges to higher prices for reserved seating or VIP experiences.

Overall, touring Munich can be tailored to fit different budgets. By planning and considering preferences for accommodation, dining, activities, and transportation, visitors can manage their expenses effectively while enjoying all that Munich has to offer.

English Speaking in Munich

In Munich, while German is the official language, English is widely spoken and understood, especially in tourist areas, hotels, restaurants, and among the younger population. Many locals, particularly in the service industry and tourist-centric areas, have a good command of English.

Here are a few things to keep in mind when speaking English in Munich:

Tourist Areas: In popular tourist spots like Marienplatz, Viktualienmarkt, or major museums, you will likely encounter English-speaking staff and signage.

Hotels and Restaurants: Staff in hotels, restaurants, and cafes often speak English and may have English menus available. However, in smaller, more traditional eateries, English proficiency might vary.

Transportation: Munich's public transport systems often have signs and announcements in English. Ticket machines typically offer language options, making it convenient for non-German speakers.

Politeness: While many locals understand English, it is respectful to greet and ask if it is okay to speak English, especially if initiating a conversation in a more local or residential area.

Learning Some German Phrases: While not necessary, knowing a few basic German phrases like "hello," "thank you," and "excuse me" can be appreciated by locals and may enhance your experience.

Patience and Courtesy: If someone does not speak English fluently, patience and politeness go a long way in communication. Speaking slowly and using simple sentences can be helpful.

Overall, English speakers can comfortably navigate Munich, as it is a cosmopolitan city accustomed to tourists from around the world. While knowing some German phrases can enhance interactions, communicating in English is generally feasible for most travelers.

Appropriate Attire While Touring Munich

While touring Munich, especially when visiting cultural sites, restaurants, or breweries, wearing smart casual attire is generally appropriate. Here are some tips:

Casual Wear: Comfortable clothing, such as jeans, trousers, skirts, or dresses, paired with T-shirts, blouses, or shirts, is suitable for most sightseeing activities.

Layers: Munich weather can vary, so layering with a light jacket or sweater is advisable, particularly in spring and autumn. If you plan to visit the mountains, South of Munich, please note, it will be much colder at the higher elevations.

Comfortable Shoes: Munich is a walkable city, so comfortable walking shoes or sneakers are essential, especially if you plan to explore the city on foot.

Respectful Clothing: If visiting religious sites or attending more formal events, it is respectful to dress modestly. This might include avoiding overly revealing clothing and opting for attire that covers shoulders and knees.

Bavarian Attire (Optional): Munich is known for its traditional clothing like Dirndls (for women) and Lederhosen (for men). While not necessary for tourists, wearing these traditional outfits can be a fun way to immerse yourself in Bavarian culture, especially during Oktoberfest or when visiting beer gardens.

Rain Gear: Munich weather can be unpredictable, so carrying a compact umbrella or a waterproof jacket can be useful, especially in spring and summer.

Overall, Munich is a cosmopolitan city where casual and smart casual attire is widely accepted in most places. However, having versatile clothing that allows you to adapt to changing weather conditions and any specific sites you plan to visit is a good strategy for a comfortable and enjoyable experience while touring the city.

Safety in Munich

Munich is known for its overall safety and relatively low crime rates compared to many other major cities. However, as with any urban area, some level of crime does exist. Here is an overview:

Low Crime Rates: Munich generally experiences low levels of violent crime. Instances of serious crimes such as assaults or homicides are relatively rare compared to other cities.

Petty Theft: The most common type of crime in Munich involves petty theft, particularly in tourist areas or crowded public spaces. Pickpocketing, especially in crowded areas like public transportation, markets, or major tourist attractions, can occur.

Precautions: To minimize the risk of petty theft, it is advisable to remain vigilant with personal belongings, especially in crowded areas. Use anti-theft bags or pouches, avoid leaving valuables unattended, and be cautious with belongings in public transport.

Safe Neighborhoods: Munich is generally safe to explore, even at night. Areas like the city center, Altstadt-Lehel, Schwabing, and Glockenbachviertel are known for their safety and vibrant atmosphere.

Police Presence: Munich has a visible police presence, and law enforcement agencies maintain the city's safety and security. Emergency services are responsive and efficient.

Scams and Frauds: Visitors should be aware of scams, such as fake charity collectors or individuals offering unwanted services for payment. Avoid engaging with strangers offering unsolicited help or services.

Drinking in Public: While public drinking is legal in Munich, excessive public drunkenness can sometimes lead to minor disturbances, especially during festivals or events like Oktoberfest.

General Safety Measures: As in any city, it is prudent to exercise common sense and caution. Stick to well-lit areas at night, use licensed taxis or ride-sharing services, and follow basic safety precautions.

Overall, Munich remains a safe destination for travelers. By taking standard safety precautions and being mindful of one's surroundings, visitors can enjoy their time in the city without major concerns about personal safety or security.

Bavarian Cuisine

Bavarian cuisine is rich and hearty, boasting a variety of flavorful dishes. Some of my favorite Bavarian food dishes include:

Weißwurst: A traditional Bavarian white sausage made with minced veal and pork back bacon, flavored with parsley, mace, onions, lemon, and cardamom. It is usually served with sweet mustard and pretzels.

Schweinshaxe: Roasted pork knuckle or ham hock with crispy skin and tender, flavorful meat. It is often accompanied by sauerkraut or potato dumplings.

Brezn (Pretzel): A quintessential Bavarian snack, these large, soft pretzels are deliciously doughy with a slightly crispy crust, best enjoyed with mustard.

Kartoffelsalat (Potato Salad): Bavarian potato salad is typically made with boiled potatoes, onions, vinegar, broth, and sometimes bacon, creating a tangy and savory side dish.

Käsespätzle: Bavaria's version of macaroni and cheese, it consists of soft egg noodles called spätzle, mixed with melted cheese, onions, and often topped with crispy fried onions.

Obatzda: A flavorful cheese spread made with Camembert, butter, onions, and spices, often served with fresh bread or pretzels.

Leberkäse: A type of savory meatloaf made from finely minced meat, usually pork and beef, mixed with spices, and baked to create a delicious slice of meat often served in sandwiches.

Apfelstrudel: A classic dessert, apple strudel is made with thinly sliced apples, cinnamon, sugar, and sometimes raisins, all wrapped in a delicate, flaky pastry.

These dishes are just a taste of the rich and comforting flavors found in Bavarian cuisine. Whether you are indulging in a hearty meal or savoring a delightful dessert, Bavarian food offers a wonderful blend of savory and sweet flavors that reflect the region's culinary traditions.

Activities in Munich (when not at the Beer Hall)

Absolutely, Munich offers a wide range of experiences and activities beyond beer-centric ones. Here are some things to enjoy in Munich if you are not inclined towards beer:

Cultural Exploration: Munich is rich in culture. Explore world-class museums like the Alte Pinakothek, Neue Pinakothek, and Pinakothek der

Moderne, which house exceptional art collections spanning various periods.

Historical Landmarks: Discover Munich's history by visiting landmarks like Marienplatz with its Glockenspiel, Frauenkirche, and Nymphenburg Palace, each offering unique insights into the city's past.

Parks and Gardens: Enjoy the tranquility of Englischer Garten, one of the world's largest urban parks, or explore the serene atmosphere of the Botanical Garden, which features a diverse range of plant species.

Culinary Exploration: Munich's gastronomy extends beyond beer. Indulge in Bavarian cuisine at traditional eateries, savoring dishes like weißwurst (white sausage), pretzels, and Schweinshaxe (roasted pork knuckle).

Shopping: Explore shopping districts like Kaufingerstraße and Maximilianstraße for a mix of high-end boutiques, department stores, and souvenir shops.

Day Trips: Munich serves as an excellent base for day trips. Visit Neuschwanstein Castle, take a trip to Salzburg, or explore the Bavarian Alps for breathtaking landscapes and outdoor activities.

Music and Theater: Enjoy performances at renowned venues like the National Theater or the

Philharmonic, highlighting classical music, opera, ballet, and more.

City Tours: Explore Munich through guided walking tours, bike tours, or hop-on-hop-off bus tours, offering insights into the city's history, architecture, and hidden gems.

Munich's diverse offerings cater to various interests, allowing visitors to immerse themselves in history, culture, nature, and entertainment beyond the beer halls and breweries. Whether you are into art, history, nature, or simply exploring the city, Munich has plenty to offer for everyone.

Non-Beer Drinks in Munich

In Munich, while beer is prominent, there is a variety of alternative drinks for those who prefer something other than beer. Here are some options to consider:

Radler or Alsterwasser: These are beer-based mixed drinks. Radler is beer mixed with lemon soda, while Alsterwasser is beer mixed with lemonade. They offer a lighter, refreshing taste than pure beer.

Apfelschorle: A popular non-alcoholic drink made by mixing apple juice with sparkling mineral water. It is widely available in cafes, restaurants, and supermarkets and is perfect for staying hydrated.

German Wines: While Bavaria is not the primary wine-producing region in Germany, you can still find a selection of local and German wines in Munich. Try Riesling, Müller-Thurgau, or Silvaner wines from nearby wine regions.

Cocktails and Spirits: Many bars and restaurants in Munich offer a wide array of cocktails and spirits. You can find classic cocktails, creative mixes, and local variations using ingredients like schnapps or herbal liqueurs.

Soft Drinks and Juices: Non-alcoholic beverages such as soft drinks, fruit juices, and mineral water are widely available in Munich, offering plenty of options for those avoiding alcohol.

Kombucha or Craft Sodas: Some cafes and health-focused establishments may offer trendy options like kombucha, or artisanal craft sodas made with natural ingredients, providing unique flavors.

Coffee and Tea: Munich has a vibrant coffee culture, with numerous cafes serving a variety of specialty coffees and teas. Enjoy a cup of German coffee or explore different tea blends available in cafes and tea houses.

While beer is a significant part of Bavarian culture, Munich's diverse culinary scene caters to various preferences. From refreshing mixed drinks and wines to a variety of non-alcoholic beverages, there

is something to suit every taste in Munich beyond
the traditional beer offerings.

Shopping in Munich

Shopping in Munich offers a delightful mix of upscale boutiques, department stores, traditional markets, and unique specialty shops. Here is a guide to shopping in Munich:

Shopping Districts:

Marienplatz and Surroundings: This central square hosts Kaufingerstraße and Neuhauser Straße, two bustling shopping streets with a mix of international brands, department stores like Kaufhof and Galeria Kaufhof, and souvenir shops.

Maximilianstraße: Known for luxury shopping, this boulevard features high-end fashion boutiques, designer labels, and upscale brands like Chanel, Louis Vuitton, and Prada.

Department Stores:

Ludwig Beck: Located at Marienplatz, this department store offers a wide range of international and local brands across multiple floors, including fashion, cosmetics, and home goods. The 5th floor contains traditional Bavarian clothes.

Kaufhof am Stachus: A large department store near Karlsplatz/Stachus offering various products, from fashion to household items.

Boutiques and Unique Shops:

Gärtnerplatzviertel: This trendy neighborhood features small boutiques, vintage stores, and specialty shops offering unique fashion, accessories, and home decor.

Schwabing: A district known for its artistic vibe, it houses independent boutiques, art galleries, and concept stores.

Traditional Bavarian Shopping:

Trachten Stores: Explore shops selling traditional Bavarian clothing like dirndls and lederhosen. Places like Angermaier and Loden-Frey offer a wide selection.

Beer Steins and Souvenirs: Visit shops around Marienplatz or Viktualienmarkt for unique souvenirs like beer steins, Bavarian crafts, and traditional gifts.

Markets:

Viktualienmarkt: A vibrant food market offering fresh produce, regional specialties, and artisanal products.

Christmas Markets: During the holiday season, Munich hosts several charming Christmas markets offering festive treats, crafts, and gifts.

Munich's shopping scene caters to diverse tastes, whether you are looking for high-end fashion, traditional Bavarian items, local specialties, or unique finds. From upscale districts to vibrant markets, there is something for every shopper to explore in Munich.

Don'ts While Visiting/Touring Munich

Absolutely, while visiting Munich, here are a few important "don'ts" to keep in mind:

Don't Jaywalk: In Munich, pedestrians tend to follow traffic signals strictly. Wait for the pedestrian lights to change before crossing the road, even if there is no traffic. If you do not, you will upset the German pedestrians around you.

Don't Forget Cash: While credit cards are widely accepted, especially in tourist areas, smaller shops, markets, or cafes might prefer cash. It is good to have some euros on hand.

Don't Be Loud in Public Places: Munich is generally peaceful, and locals appreciate quiet public spaces. Avoid being overly loud, especially in parks or residential areas. No noise on Sundays!

Don't Assume Everyone Speaks English: While many people in Munich speak English, it is courteous to begin conversations with a greeting in German and ask if the person speaks English.

Don't Touch the Art: When visiting museums or galleries, avoid touching the exhibits, even if they seem accessible. Respect the art and follow the displayed guidelines.

Don't Ignore Recycling Rules: Munich takes recycling seriously. Be mindful of separating waste into designated bins for paper, plastic, glass, and organic waste as indicated.

Don't Be Impolite in Beer Halls: If you are in a traditional beer hall, it is customary to find a table and sit rather than standing. Also, do not move someone else's belongings if they have reserved a table.

Don't Forget to Tip Appropriately: While tipping is not as obligatory as in some other countries, rounding up the bill or leaving a small tip (5-10%) for good service is appreciated in restaurants and cafes.

Don't Disrespect Cultural Norms: Respect local customs and traditions, especially in religious sites or during festivals. Dress modestly in churches and follow the rules of conduct in cultural spaces.

Observing these 'don'ts' can help ensure a respectful and enjoyable experience during your stay in Munich. It is always a good idea to familiarize yourself with local customs and etiquette to make the most of your visit.

Beer Hall Putsch of 1923

The "Hitler beer hall" refers to the Bürgerbräukeller beer hall in Munich, which gained notoriety due to its historical significance in relation to Adolf Hitler and the Nazi Party.

The Bürgerbräukeller was a prominent beer hall where Hitler delivered early speeches during the rise of the Nazi Party in the 1920s. One of the most significant events associated with this venue was the failed Beer Hall Putsch of 1923. Hitler and his supporters attempted to overthrow the Bavarian government but were met with resistance. The coup failed, and Hitler was arrested and subsequently imprisoned, during which time he wrote his manifesto, Mein Kampf.

The Bürgerbräukeller remained a gathering place for Nazi sympathizers and supporters throughout the 1930s, serving as a venue for Hitler's speeches and rallies. However, during World War II, in 1944, the beer hall was heavily damaged by an Allied bombing raid and was eventually demolished in the 1960s.

Today, while the original Bürgerbräukeller no longer exists, its historical significance remains notable in discussions about the early days of Hitler's political career and the rise of the Nazi Party in Munich. The location holds historical memory but has been replaced by new developments over the years. The location is at a S-Bahn staircase next to the Hilton Hotel on Rosenheimer Platz.

History and Facts of Munich

Munich, the capital of Bavaria in southern Germany, has a rich and diverse history that dates back centuries. Here are key milestones in the history of Munich:

Foundation: Munich was founded in 1158 by Henry the Lion, Duke of Bavaria, who established a bridge across the Isar River, where the city's name originated from "München" or "by the monks' place."

Bavarian Seat of Power: In 1255, Munich became the official residence of the Wittelsbach dynasty, rulers of Bavaria. Over time, the city grew in importance as a center of power and commerce.

Cultural and Economic Development: Throughout the Renaissance and Baroque periods, Munich flourished culturally and economically, marked by the construction of iconic landmarks like the Frauenkirche and Theatine Church.

Royal Legacy: The 19th century saw Munich become a center of arts and culture under the reign of King Ludwig I. His passion for arts led to the construction of grand boulevards, neoclassical architecture, and notable institutions like the Glyptothek and Alte Pinakothek.

Beer Culture: Munich's beer culture has deep historical roots, marked by the establishment of beer halls and breweries. The Oktoberfest celebration began in 1810 with the marriage celebration of King Ludwig I and Princess Therese.

World Wars and Rebuilding: Munich faced destruction during World War II but underwent significant reconstruction in the post-war period, contributing to its modern development as an economic and cultural hub.

Modern Munich: Today, Munich stands as a vibrant city known for its economic strength, technological innovation, world-class museums, and a blend of traditional Bavarian culture with modern amenities.

Throughout its history, Munich has experienced periods of cultural renaissance, political power, devastation, and growth, contributing to its unique identity as a city that blends history with contemporary vitality.

1972 Summer Olympic Games

The 1972 Summer Olympics, officially known as the Games of the XX Olympiad, were held in Munich, Germany, from August 26th to September 11th, 1972. The Munich Games were the second Olympics held in Germany after the 1936 Berlin Games.

Key aspects of the 1972 Olympics:

Tragic Events: The Games were overshadowed by a tragic event known as the Munich Massacre. Palestinian terrorists from the group "Black September" infiltrated the Olympic Village, taking Israeli athletes' hostage. Ultimately, 11 Israeli athletes and coaches, as well as a German police officer, lost their lives in a failed rescue attempt at the military airport of Fürstenfeldbruck.

Sports and Achievements: Despite the tragedy, the sporting events continued. The 1972 Olympics featured impressive athletic achievements and notable performances, including Mark Spitz's seven gold medals in swimming and Soviet gymnast Olga Korbut's captivating performances.

Memorable Moments: The Games witnessed the introduction of several events, such as basketball for women, water polo for women, and handball. It also marked the return of South Africa to the Olympics after a 12-year absence due to apartheid.

Controversies and Legacy: The Munich Games were marred not only by the tragedy but also by controversies, including disputes over judging in various sports. Despite the grim events, the Games left a legacy in terms of advancements in sports facilities, technology, and the integration of women's events.

The 1972 Munich Olympics are remembered both for the moments of sporting excellence and the tragic events that cast a shadow over the celebration of athletic achievement. The Games highlighted the vulnerability of large-scale international events to security threats and had a profound impact on future Olympics in terms of security measures and protocols.

Sports in Munich

Munich, being a vibrant city in Germany, offers a diverse range of sports activities and opportunities for enthusiasts and athletes. Here are some key aspects of sports in Munich:

Football (Soccer): Football holds a special place in Munich's sports culture. The city is home to two prominent football clubs: FC Bayern Munich, one of the most successful clubs in Europe, and TSV 1860 Munich. The Allianz Arena, shared by Bayern Munich and 1860 Munich, is a major venue for football matches and events.

Olympic Legacy: Munich hosted the 1972 Summer Olympics and still benefits from the sports facilities built for the Games. The Olympic Park remains a hub for sports and leisure activities, offering facilities for athletics, swimming, cycling, and more. The iconic Olympiaturm (Olympic Tower) provides panoramic views of the city.

Outdoor Activities: Munich's surrounding landscape is ideal for outdoor sports. The Isar River provides opportunities for kayaking, paddleboarding, and river surfing. Nearby Bavarian Alps offer hiking, skiing, and mountaineering options.

Running and Cycling: The city boasts numerous parks and green spaces, including Englischer

Garten, perfect for jogging, running, and cycling. The extensive network of bike lanes encourages cycling as a popular means of transportation and leisure.

Winter Sports: During winter, nearby Alpine resorts such as Garmisch-Partenkirchen offer skiing, snowboarding, and other winter sports activities, easily accessible from Munich.

Traditional Bavarian Sports: Munich embraces traditional Bavarian sports like Schuhplattler (folk dance), Eisstockschießen (ice stock sport), and others, often celebrated during cultural festivals and events.

Golf: Munich features several golf courses, attracting enthusiasts who enjoy the sport in scenic surroundings.

Fitness and Gyms: The city offers a wide range of fitness centers, gyms, and sports clubs catering to various fitness levels and interests.

Munich's sports scene is diverse, offering opportunities for both spectators and active participants across various sports, from professional football to outdoor activities, catering to a broad spectrum of interests and fitness levels.

German Football in Munich

Football holds a special place in Munich's cultural fabric, and the city is home to two prominent football clubs:

FC Bayern Munich: One of the most successful and internationally renowned football clubs globally. Bayern Munich has a storied history, having won numerous domestic and international titles, including multiple Bundesliga titles and UEFA Champions League trophies. The team plays its home matches at the Allianz Arena, a modern and iconic stadium.

TSV 1860 Munich: Another traditional Munich-based football club, known as "Die Löwen" (The Lions). While not as consistently successful as Bayern Munich, TSV 1860 has its own passionate fan base and has had its share of achievements in German football history. They previously shared the Allianz Arena with Bayern but now play in the third tier of German football.

Football in Munich goes beyond the matches themselves; it is deeply ingrained in the city's social life and culture. The local fans are passionate, creating an electric atmosphere during matches, especially derby games between Bayern Munich and TSV 1860 Munich or during international competitions like the UEFA Champions League.

The Allianz Arena, with its distinctive architecture and capacity to hold over 75,000 spectators, serves as a hub for football enthusiasts. Visitors to Munich often try to catch a match at this renowned stadium to experience the city's football culture firsthand.

Churches in Munich

Munich is home to several beautiful and historically significant churches that display stunning architecture and cultural heritage. Some of the famous churches in Munich include:

Frauenkirche (Cathedral of Our Dear Lady): This iconic landmark is Munich's most recognizable church, characterized by its twin onion-domed towers. It is one of the largest Gothic churches in southern Germany and offers impressive views from its towers.

St. Peter's Church (Peterskirche): Located near Marienplatz, St. Peter's Church is Munich's oldest parish church. Visitors can climb the tower for panoramic views of the city.

Theatine Church (Theatinerkirche St. Kajetan): Known for its stunning baroque architecture, this church was commissioned by Elector Ferdinand Maria and his wife in the 17th century. It features a distinctive yellow facade and impressive interior decorations.

Asam Church (Asamkirche St. Johann Nepomuk): Often referred to as the Asam Church, this small baroque gem was built by the Asam brothers, artists, and architects, as their private church. Its interior is lavishly decorated.

The Ludwigskirche: Constructed in the early 19th century, this church is a prime example of neoclassical architecture in Munich. Its monumental appearance and impressive interior make it a notable landmark.

All Saints Church (Allerheiligen-Hofkirche): This church, part of the Munich Residenz complex, features a mix of Renaissance and Baroque styles. It served as the private chapel for the Bavarian royal family.

St. Michael's Church (Michaelkirche): A Renaissance-style church that underwent Baroque renovations, St. Michael's is known for its impressive altar and tomb of King Ludwig II.

These churches not only serve as places of worship but also stand as architectural and historical landmarks, contributing to Munich's rich cultural heritage and attracting visitors from around the world. Each church has its unique architectural style, historical significance, and artistic elements worth exploring.

Munich During and After WWII

During World War II, Munich, like many other cities in Germany, experienced significant destruction due to bombings and the ravages of war. Here is an overview of Munich's history during and after the war:

War Period (1939-1945): Munich was a key target for Allied bombings due to its industrial importance and ties to the Nazi regime. The city suffered considerable damage, especially in the later stages of the war. Many historical buildings, including churches and landmarks, were destroyed or heavily damaged.

Munich as a Nazi Stronghold: Munich held significance in Nazi history. The city was central to the rise of the Nazi Party, where Adolf Hitler first joined and later established the party headquarters, the Brown House (Braunes Haus).

Post-War Reconstruction: After the war, Munich underwent extensive rebuilding efforts to restore the city's infrastructure and reconstruct damaged buildings. The reconstruction focused on restoring historical landmarks while also incorporating modern architectural elements.

Recovery and Economic Growth: Munich experienced a rapid recovery and economic growth in the post-war period. The city's economy diversified into various sectors, including technology, finance, and manufacturing, contributing to its resurgence.

Refugees and Displacement: The aftermath of the war saw a significant influx of refugees and displaced persons seeking shelter and stability in Munich. The city provided housing and support as part of the broader efforts for post-war rehabilitation.

Cultural Renaissance: Despite the war's devastation, Munich experienced a cultural revival in the post-war years. The city rekindled its reputation as a cultural center, nurturing art, music, and literature.

Olympic Games 1972: In a poignant moment of symbolic healing, Munich hosted the 1972 Summer Olympics, marking the city's transformation and highlighting its revival from the scars of war.

Munich's journey during and after World War II reflects the resilience of its residents and the city's determination to rebuild and thrive. Today, Munich stands as a vibrant, modern city, while still preserving its historical heritage, marking a testament to its resilience and recovery from the war's devastation.

Day Trips from Munich

Munich's central location in Bavaria offers a myriad of fascinating day trip options to explore the surrounding areas. Here are some popular day trip destinations from Munich:

Neuschwanstein Castle: One of the most iconic and picturesque castles in the world, located near Füssen. This fairy-tale-like castle was the inspiration for Disney's Sleeping Beauty Castle.

Salzburg, Austria: Mozart's birthplace and a UNESCO World Heritage Site, Salzburg is a charming city with a rich musical heritage, stunning architecture, and beautiful landscapes.

Eagle's Nest (Kehlsteinhaus): Once Hitler's mountain retreat, this historical site offers breathtaking views of the Bavarian Alps and an intriguing glimpse into history.

Dachau Concentration Camp Memorial Site: A somber but important historical site, the memorial provides insights into the atrocities of the Nazi regime and honors the victims of the Holocaust.

Nuremberg: Known for its medieval architecture, Nuremberg offers attractions like the Imperial Castle, the historic Old Town, and the Documentation Center Nazi Party Rally Grounds.

Herrenchiemsee Palace: Another palace built by King Ludwig II, situated on Herreninsel in Lake Chiemsee. It is a replica of the Palace of Versailles and displays grandeur and opulence.

Andechs Monastery: A Benedictine monastery famous for its brewery and beer garden. Visitors can tour the monastery, enjoy scenic views, and taste the monastery's beer.

Garmisch-Partenkirchen: A picturesque town nestled in the Bavarian Alps, offering outdoor activities like hiking, skiing, and visiting the famous Partnach Gorge.

Regensburg: A beautifully preserved medieval town with a UNESCO-listed Old Town, notable for its historic stone bridge, cathedral, and vibrant cultural scene.

These destinations, each within a few hours' drive or accessible by train from Munich, offer a diverse range of experiences, from historical and cultural sites to breathtaking natural landscapes, making for enriching day trips from the city.

Family Friendly Activities in Munich

Munich offers plenty of family-friendly activities and attractions that cater to children. Here are some fun things to do in Munich with kids:

English Garden (Englischer Garten): Explore this expansive park with numerous playgrounds, a Japanese teahouse, streams for paddling, and even a popular spot for river surfing at the Eisbach.

Deutsches Museum: One of the world's largest science and technology museums, offering interactive exhibits, demonstrations, and hands-on activities suitable for kids of all ages.

Hellabrunn Zoo: Munich's beloved zoo, offering a wide variety of animals in naturalistic habitats. It also has a petting zoo and various play areas.

Olympiapark: Visit this park built for the 1972 Olympics, offering a range of activities such as biking, skating, and playgrounds. The highlight is the Olympiaturm with its observation deck providing panoramic views.

SEA LIFE Munich: A fascinating aquarium located in the Olympiapark, featuring diverse marine life, interactive touch pools, and educational exhibits.

Bavaria Filmstadt (Bavaria Film Studios): Explore behind the scenes of movie magic with guided tours that display film sets, props, and special effects. Kids can enjoy interactive activities and experiences.

Children's Museum (Kindermuseum): A museum designed specifically for children, offering hands-on experiences, workshops, and interactive exhibits focusing on art, science, and culture.

Nymphenburg Palace: Explore the vast grounds, visit the palace, and enjoy the beautiful gardens ideal for picnics and leisurely walks.

Glyptothek and Alte Pinakothek: Introduce children to art at these museums housing impressive collections of sculptures and paintings. They often have family-friendly programs and guided tours.

Miniature Railway in the Westpark: Kids can ride on the small train through Westpark, a beautifully landscaped park, offering a fun experience for young children.

Munich's diverse offerings cater to families with children, providing a blend of educational, recreational, and cultural experiences to make the visit enjoyable for kids of all ages.

Accessibilities and Accommodations for Disabilities

Touring Munich while managing disabilities requires thoughtful planning to ensure accessibility and enjoyable experiences. Here are some tips and considerations for disabled travelers visiting Munich:

Accessible Transportation: Munich has an extensive public transportation system, including buses, trams, and the subway (U-Bahn) with accessible options. Look for low-floor trams and buses or use the accessible entrances at U-Bahn stations.

Wheelchair-Friendly Attractions: Many of Munich's main attractions, such as museums and landmarks like the Frauenkirche or Nymphenburg Palace, have provisions for wheelchair access and aid disabled visitors.

Accessible Accommodations: Prioritize booking hotels or accommodations that offer accessible rooms and facilities, including ramps, elevators, and accessible bathrooms.

Accessible Tours: Look for guided tours or city tours that cater to disabled travelers, offering accessible transportation and tailored experiences for those with mobility issues.

Munich City Pass: Consider purchasing a Munich City Pass or Card, which often includes free or discounted access to attractions and public transport, potentially saving money while exploring the city.

Advance Planning and Information: Research attractions and contact them in advance to inquire about accessibility, available facilities, and any specific assistance they offer for disabled visitors.

Accessible Restaurants and Cafés: Look for restaurants and eateries that provide wheelchair access and comfortable seating arrangements for disabled individuals.

Assistance Services: Consider using local mobility and assistance services specifically designed for disabled tourists, such as accessible taxi services or rental equipment for mobility aids.

Pavements and Streets: Be aware that some parts of Munich might have cobblestone streets or uneven pavements, which could pose challenges for wheelchair users or those with mobility difficulties.

Take Breaks and Rest: Pace yourself and plan breaks to rest when needed, ensuring a more comfortable and enjoyable experience while exploring Munich.

Prior research, planning, and communicating specific needs with relevant venues or services can greatly enhance the experience of touring Munich for disabled travelers, ensuring accessibility and an enjoyable visit.

LGBTQ+ in Munich

Munich, like many major cities in Germany, has a diverse and inclusive LGBTQ+ community with various resources and establishments that cater to the community's needs. Here are some aspects of the LGBTQ+ scene in Munich:

Gay Scene: Munich has a vibrant LGBTQ+ scene with gay bars, clubs, and cafes primarily concentrated in the Glockenbachviertel district. This area is known for its LGBTQ+ friendly establishments and a lively nightlife.

Events and Festivals: Munich hosts the annual Pride Parade, known as Christopher Street Day (CSD) in July, celebrating LGBTQ+ rights, diversity, and inclusion. It is a major event drawing participants and supporters from across Germany and beyond.

Support Organizations: There are several LGBTQ+ support organizations, community centers, and counseling services in Munich, offering resources, advocacy, and support for LGBTQ+ individuals.

Inclusive Spaces: Munich prides itself on being an inclusive city. Many establishments, including bars, restaurants, and cultural venues, are welcoming and supportive of LGBTQ+ patrons.

Legal Rights: Germany, including Munich, has made significant strides in LGBTQ+ rights. Same-sex marriage has been legal since 2017, granting equal rights in adoption, tax benefits, and spousal rights.

Acceptance and Tolerance: Munich generally has a progressive and tolerant attitude towards the LGBTQ+ community. However, as with any city, individual attitudes may vary.

Diversity in Culture and Arts: Munich's cultural landscape often includes LGBTQ+ themes and events in arts, films, and theater, contributing to a more inclusive cultural environment.

Museums and Art Galleries in Munich

Munich boasts a rich cultural heritage with a variety of world-class museums and art galleries highlighting diverse collections. Here are some famous art and museums in Munich:

Alte Pinakothek: Known for its extensive collection of European paintings from the Middle Ages to the end of the Rococo period. It features works by renowned artists like Rubens, DaVinci, Rembrandt, and Dürer.

Neue Pinakothek: Focuses on European art from the 18th to the early 20th century, displaying works from the Romantic period to Impressionism, including pieces by Van Gogh, Monet, and Gauguin.

Pinakothek der Moderne: A modern art museum housing collections of modern and contemporary art, design, architecture, and works by artists like Kandinsky, Picasso, and Warhol.

Glyptothek: This museum is dedicated to ancient sculpture, housing Greek and Roman sculptures, including the iconic Barberini Faun and the figures from the Temple of Aphaia on Aegina.

Lenbachhaus: Known for its collection of works by the artists of the "Blaue Reiter" group, including Kandinsky and Münter. It also highlights Munich School paintings and contemporary art.

Museum Brandhorst: Focuses on contemporary art and features works by notable artists like Cy Twombly, Andy Warhol, and Damien Hirst, among others.

Deutsches Museum: One of the world's largest science and technology museums, covering various fields such as aerospace, transportation, natural sciences, and technology.

BMW Museum: Showcases the history, technology, and innovation of BMW cars and motorcycles through interactive exhibits and displays.

Haus der Kunst: An art museum hosting temporary exhibitions of contemporary art, photography, and installations.

Documentation Center for the History of National Socialism: A museum dedicated to Munich's role in the rise of the Nazi Party, providing historical insights and exhibitions about the era.

These museums and art galleries in Munich offer diverse collections, from ancient sculptures to modern and contemporary art, providing a comprehensive cultural experience for art enthusiasts and visitors interested in history, science, and innovation.

Entertainment in Munich

Munich offers a wide range of entertainment options catering to various tastes and interests. Here are some popular entertainment choices in the city:

Theater and Opera: Munich is renowned for its world-class theaters and opera houses, such as the National Theatre (Residenztheater), the Bavarian State Opera (Bayerische Staatsoper), and the Gärtnerplatz Theater, highlighting opera, ballet, and theater productions.

Live Music: The city has a vibrant live music scene with venues offering diverse genres, including classical music, jazz clubs, rock, indie, and electronic music. Places like the Philharmonie, Olympiahalle, and smaller clubs host performances by local and international artists.

Museums and Art Galleries: Munich boasts numerous museums and art galleries catering to various interests, from classical art at the Alte and Neue Pinakothek to contemporary art at the Pinakothek der Moderne and exhibitions at the Haus der Kunst.

Beer Gardens and Halls: Munich's beer gardens and beer halls offer not just great brews but also a lively atmosphere with traditional music, dancing,

and conviviality, especially during events like
Oktoberfest.

Cultural Events and Festivals: The city hosts a
variety of cultural events and festivals throughout
the year, including the famous Oktoberfest,
Tollwood Festival, Filmfest München, and the
Munich Opera Festival.

Parks and Recreation: Munich has beautiful
parks like the Englischer Garten and Olympiapark,
offering opportunities for outdoor activities, picnics,
and relaxation. Olympiapark also hosts events,
concerts, and sports activities.

Shopping and Dining: The city's diverse
shopping districts cater to different styles and
budgets, while the culinary scene boasts traditional
Bavarian cuisine, international flavors, and
Michelin-starred restaurants.

Sports and Activities: Munich provides various
sports activities, from watching professional
football matches at Allianz Arena to participating in
outdoor activities like cycling, hiking, and winter
sports in nearby alpine regions.

Nightlife: Munich has a lively nightlife scene with
bars, clubs, and cocktail lounges, especially around
the Glockenbachviertel and Schwabing districts,
offering a mix of trendy spots and classic beer
halls.

Munich's diverse entertainment options ensure there is something for everyone, whether it is exploring cultural heritage, enjoying live performances, experiencing the local beer culture, or indulging in outdoor activities.

Tourist Traps in Munich

In Munich, while there are many wonderful attractions and experiences to enjoy, some places might be considered tourist traps, often due to high prices, crowds, or over-commercialization. Here are a few spots that could fall into that category:

Marienplatz: While Marienplatz is a central square and home to the famous Glockenspiel, it can get very crowded with tourists, and the surrounding restaurants and shops may have higher prices due to its prime location.

Hofbräuhaus: Although iconic and a must-visit for many, the Hofbräuhaus can sometimes feel overcrowded and touristy. The atmosphere may cater more to tourists than locals, leading to higher prices and a less authentic experience.

Viktualienmarkt: While a fantastic market with fresh produce, local food, and Bavarian specialties, it has become increasingly popular with tourists, resulting in higher prices and sometimes a less genuine local feel.

Dachau Concentration Camp Memorial Site: While historically significant and essential for learning, some visitors might find it crowded and potentially overwhelming due to its somber nature.

Hop-On Hop-Off Bus Tours: While convenient for seeing many sights in a short time, these tours can be pricey and might not offer a deep, immersive experience of the city.

It is important to note that these places might be considered touristy but can still offer valuable experiences. It is often about managing expectations and embracing the aspects that appeal to you while being mindful of potential downsides such as crowds and inflated prices. Exploring off-the-beaten-path areas and seeking recommendations from locals can also enhance your Munich experience.

Famous Citizens of Munich

Munich has been home to various influential and notable individuals across different fields. Here are some famous people associated with Munich:

Werner Heisenberg: A pioneering physicist and Nobel laureate known for his contributions to quantum mechanics. He was born in Würzburg but spent a significant part of his career in Munich.

Gustav Mahler: A renowned composer and conductor of the late Romantic period, Mahler served as the director of the Munich Court Opera from 1908 to 1910.

Ludwig Maximilian University of Munich (LMU) Figures: Several influential scholars and scientists associated with LMU Munich, one of Europe's leading research universities, have lived and worked in Munich, contributing significantly to their respective fields.

Franz Beckenbauer: A legendary footballer known for his achievements with Bayern Munich and the German national team. Beckenbauer is widely regarded as one of the greatest footballers of all time.

Rainer Werner Fassbinder: A prominent film director, screenwriter, and playwright associated with the New German Cinema movement.

Fassbinder's innovative work in cinema gained international recognition.

Georg Baselitz: A renowned contemporary artist known for his distinctive style and contributions to the Neo-Expressionist movement. Baselitz was born in Deutschbaselitz, which is near Munich.

Thomas Mann: Though born in Lübeck, the Nobel Prize-winning author lived in Munich and portrayed the city in some of his literary works. He is known for novels like "Buddenbrooks" and "The Magic Mountain."

Gloria von Thurn und Taxis: A prominent socialite and businesswoman known for her extravagant lifestyle and philanthropic endeavors. She resides in the Thurn und Taxis Palace in Regensburg, but her family has historical ties to Munich.

These individuals, among others, have left lasting legacies in their respective fields and have connections to Munich, contributing to the city's cultural, scientific, and artistic heritage.

In Closing

Exploring beer tourism in Munich, Germany, offers an immersive journey into the heart of Bavarian brewing heritage. From iconic beer halls like the Hofbräuhaus to traditional breweries like Augustiner and Paulaner, Munich presents a tapestry of experiences for beer enthusiasts.

Embark on brewery tours to witness centuries-old techniques, savor authentic Bavarian flavors, and delve into the artistry of beer-making. Whether enjoying a stein in a historic beer hall, savoring regional specialties in a beer garden, or learning the craft behind Munich's iconic brews, beer tourism in Munich intertwines history, culture, and conviviality.

Immerse yourself in the sights, sounds, and tastes of this beer-loving city, where every sip tells a story, and every brewery visit reveals a new chapter in Munich's enduring beer culture. Prost to the unparalleled experience of beer tourism in Munich, where every pint is a celebration of tradition, craftsmanship, and Bavarian hospitality.

About the Author

Paris Finch is a writer, composer and musican that is a founding member of the rock band, Songbomb. Paris is an experienced world traveler with much time spend indulging in the customers and cultures of many different locations and people. He is a resident of Wyomissing, Pennsylvania, USA.

www.ingramcontent.com/pod-product-compliance
Lightning Source LLC
LaVergne TN
LVHW022053190726
843495LV00014B/1758